22 Days

IN THE COUNTY JAIL

The Cautionary Tale of a Suburban Housewife

DEBORAH LOVETT

Published by ROOTED Publishing for Kindle Direct Publishing
Cover designed by ROOTED Publishing

ISBN: 9781797644929

DEDICATION

This book is dedicated to those considered "one of the least of these" (Matthew 25:40, New International Version): those who have been hurt by abuse (mental or emotional), held captive behind the bars of a physical or emotional prison, or those who have ever felt like no one loves them.

May you see the lies, and replace them with truth and hope.

You are a remarkable person.

You are not alone.

You are loved.

You are.

Especially for:

Mike, Luke and Jake

We have never stopped loving you

CONTENTS

PROLOGUE

You are about to enter into the nightmare of a seemingly ordinary suburban housewife who spent 22 days in the County Jail. In this haunting tale, every woman can find herself: whether religious or not, sober or addict, married or single, abused or loved, forgiven or forgotten, perfect or imperfect, desperate or delivered. The time you spend here is not for the faint at heart. You will go from eating home cooked meals, to bug-infested donuts; from sleeping on soft warm linens, to the thin hard mat on a cold cement floor; from wearing full length furs to jailhouse orange; from knowing all the right answers, to losing sight of everything; from marriage to divorce; and ultimately from death to life or life to death, depending on how you look at it.

My friend's diary will not compare to the domestic diva, Martha Stewart's prison tabloids, the popular heiress, Paris Hilton's jail cell notes, or the notorious Lindsey Lohan's exploits in and out of

1

jail. However, you will find a depth that will inspire you, make you cry and hopefully even give you a few laughs. Like the old proverb says, "Laughter is good medicine for the soul!"

The characters range from the expletive-speaking guards to women of every age and culture; guilty (and some not-so-guilty) of everything from cold-blooded murder to simply not paying their court fines.

As we journey through jail with her we will begin by spending time in segregation then in maximum security, and ending in the free for all dorm. Believe me when I tell you that her diary is an eye-opening look at what goes on inside a county jail from the pen of a suburban housewife. Having never been inside a county jail myself, I came away feeling like I had just visited hell.

Finally, I, Deb, communicate to you anticipating that meaning will be given to the often untold suffering many women face today, perhaps not only in county jails, but often in their very own living rooms. Perhaps through some spiritual seed, courage will be birthed to women through my friend's account. I pray that it will motivate women-at-risk to see the light and begin to reach out to safe women who are willing to start forming protective circles around them and vice versa. On a more personal note I write to give my friend a voice. This is also my own way of helping her find some victory through the pearls of pain woven through her own life.

Now, though this is a short memoir based on a true-life drama, some names have been changed in order to protect the innocent and the guilty. The ticket to engaging yourself comes from reading with your heart, not your mind. By doing so you will soon start to feel the heartbeat of one of my best friends ever, the suburban housewife, Bridgett.

THE SUBURBAN HOUSEWIFE

Desperate housewives need to be loved

Please allow me the pleasure and honor of introducing you to my girlfriend, Bridgett, who was three years younger than I. First of all, she had quite the sense of humor and loved to laugh. Yet on the other hand, she was full of mercy, laid back and relaxed. She could easily have won the Miss Congeniality award for her charm, quick wit and bubbling personality. If you are picturing Sandra Bullock right about now, you are on the right track.

She also had the most gorgeous, ocean blue eyes you have ever laid eyes on. (No pun intended.) They reminded me a little like Barbara Eden's eyes, from the television show, I Dream of Jeannie. They seemed to connect directly to your soul when they looked at you. At times you might even think if she twitched her nose you were headed for trouble! Other times they darted off quickly in different directions, barely noticing your presence at all, leaving you wondering what in the world she was thinking about in some strange, mysterious way.

Her essence was that of a woman who was sensitive, warm, loving, and ever so giving. Overall, she was absolutely charming. She could charm the socks off any man, or woman for that matter.

Our childhood was packed full of happy memories with us playing kickball or tag in the alley behind our humble dwellings we called home. Since we lived next door to each other, we practically lived at each other's houses. Many times we shared my small bedroom when I had sleepovers. She was the messy one, and I was neat and tidy, so it just about drove me crazy to have her spend the night. However we really didn't have anything to complain about as we both had a roof over our heads, meat and potatoes for dinner every night (that we were expected to finish,) and clothes that were usually handed down by one of my sisters or sewn with love by her sister Toria. In our pre-school days, I would play the stoic teacher, and she would be my fidgety student. In our elementary days, I advanced to giving her piano lessons. (She never took up music after that.) So overall our childhood was pretty ordinary, nothing tragic happened; or if it did we never found out about it, as we were too busy playing without a care in the world. My parents always seemed to save enough money so we could vacation in Florida every summer and Bridgett usually joined us, as we were inseparable. All that to say: when we were growing up, Bridgett had a contented and joyful disposition, never asked for much, never complained. I do remember her having to take some orange colored epileptic medicine everyday though. She would let me take it once in a while when her mom wasn't looking because it tasted so good.

By high school, she was a great gymnast all by herself, without my mentoring~ as I could not even touch my toes. She was the only person I knew that could smile the kind of smile you see on toothpaste commercials while doing a back bend all at the same time. Not only was she talented but she was also double jointed.

At the beginning of my freshman year in High School her parents moved her to the nicer side of town many people call suburbia. I would drive over and we would jog around the block in the evenings when we could find the time to do so. That was our time as friends when we really connected again and shared our struggles as teenagers.

After both attending Catholic elementary and private Catholic High Schools, Bridgett then went on to college at Miami University where she received her Bachelor's degree in International Business, graduating with a total of five, yes, five, languages under her belt. I believe she could even write Japanese. She could multitask amazingly well. She partied right alongside the best of them as she sailed through college with flying colors, usually with some buff guy lined up for Friday night and a party with the girls on Saturday night. It was fun catching up when she returned home for breaks.

Bridgett's lifelong dream was to be married, have children, a white picket fence, a husband to love, and to be loved back. Now really, isn't that all we really want when it comes right down to it? Someone to love us back. Love is one thing we all have in common.

Love motivates us, sustains us, and it is a powerful thing if it is birthed from a heart with right motives. Sometimes though, when abused, it can compel a woman to do things they never imagined they were capable of doing. Bridgett was one of those women. She searched for love and at one point found what she thought was love...

I remember her special day like it was yesterday. I, of course, was in the wedding! All her friends and family were there and the celebration was underway. It was a huge wedding, complete with the traditional white Cinderella bridal gown, a rather small diamond ring, tons of bridesmaids, groomsmen, alcohol, food and all the dancing you could imagine! Nothing was missing. Everything was perfect. It truly was a day to remember and she was the princess! I can still smell the aroma of the dew dropped yellow roses in every nook and cranny of the reception hall. Yellow and purple were Bridgett's very favorite colors.

Moving forward in your mind's eye, take Bridgett and her new husband and place them in a good-looking manicured and symmetrically tree lined suburban neighborhood just outside Chicago in a quaint little town with children of every age and size playing outdoors. If you have ever watched the television show, Desperate Housewives, you are probably picturing Wisteria Lane right about now. And just like most upper income suburban neighborhoods, their street housed a variety of different characters ranging from: some men toting their golf clubs to the nearest country club, some working late hours, women spending the day shopping and getting pampered at the spa, others getting ready to put their fur on for a night of fine dining and wines, all while the Au Pairs took over the child watch. Yet others were doing things behind closed doors that no one ever dreamed of, much like many of the reality shows on television today.

Most of the time Bridgett was at home caring for her own children and the neighbors too. She always tried to be mom of the year. She was born to be a mother and she could show me up any day of the week. I had never witnessed a love quite like hers, involved in every aspect of her children's lives. She began knowing what she wanted and respecting herself. She drove a mini-van, had twin boys, and tried to juggle life with joy and her usual humor. And yes, although she had to marry and move away to get it, she finally had her very own dream home: Victorian style, with a huge white wrap around porch, complete with gingerbread moldings and of course, a hanging porch swing and white picket fence! It seemed as if all was good, really good. Could it be the perfect all-American dream up close and personal? Or was it just an idyllic mirage?

At first my childhood friend and her husband came home to visit quite often, and then less and less frequently after she gave birth to her adorable twins. Then, when they did travel home, children in tow, it seemed as if most of their time was spent at his mother's house. I know this doesn't happen often, but in a perfect world, the man should honor his mother, and by doing so, he will naturally put his wife above his mother at the time of marriage, not by forsaking his mother, but by putting his wife first. This would mean sharing time between families, not isolating her from a family she loved dearly.

After a while, Bridgett rarely visited her own family or me and my family. I should have known then that something was not quite right. Have you ever noticed how sometimes we just let things go, when we really should be checking into them? I guess we think it is easier not to get involved? Or perhaps we think we are just imagining things? Perhaps we think it is not our responsibility? Or are we just too busy? Eventually, even our frequent phone calls to each other became sporadic. I figured the separation between us was just the season of life we were both in. After all, we were both busy, married with children, living in suburbia. She in Chicago and I in Ohio.

Looking back, perhaps it was the loneliness combined with the responsibility of raising not only two but eventually three boys that started her down the path of no return. Loneliness is an epidemic these days. People just don't connect relationally like they used to. Think about it--with all the I Phones, I Pads, and Podcasts —most communication these days is done in a very impersonal manner. Even many married couples run their marriages like a business these days, merely passing each other in the hall and nodding. Did you know the #1 predictor of divorce is emotional distance between couples? Some couples go all day without talking, but will text and email each other without thinking twice about the other person, while checking things off their lists, and then checking their profit and loss statement at the same time. Loneliness can lead to desperation; and desperation usually leads us to sinful choices, and eventually a dead end. We need to guard against it. More infiltration and less isolation are key. Unity is a gift that must be either maintained or lost. Okay, I will quit preaching.

It's hard to sum someone's life up in a few pages. Especially someone you shared all your childhood with, tried to help, and love and miss so very much. But here is what I think of when memories flood my mind of my best buddy: I see her playing ball with her three boys, reading to them, fishing at the nearby lake, riding bikes, baking cookies, pouring out her love to them and dressing them in their Sunday best for church. She had an incredible knack of being a child herself when she was with them. Finally, I imagine her tucking those boys in each and every night with love. She loved those boys more than life itself. And yes, I do believe her love was as pure as a mother's love gets.

FROM FAIRY TALE TO FAILURE

Silence is not always golden.

I cannot narrow it down to one simple thing that happened in their 15-year marriage to start the love-hate relationship they seemed to juggle. All I know is whatever it was, it grew and brewed until it was a deadly cocktail.

At first sight they seemed to be a match made in heaven. They had the fairy tale beginning. He would have walked through hot coals for her and she for him. I had never witnessed such a lovey-dovey couple in all my life. It was almost sickening, if you know what I mean. I realize now that it was too much, too soon. Sad how some things can start out seemingly sound and end up miserable and rotten. My guess is that their dating days were their best days ever.

In her personal diary she wrote that her marriage started with long days of silence between them, no talking, just tension. Those times continued throughout their marriage. Silence. More avoidance.

No talking. Eventually, I imagine the anger and bitterness that built up during those continuous episodes must have been unbearable. God warns us to not let the sun go down on our anger and I believe it is for our own good as well as for those we love. Anger can eat away at you like cancer. We have to change the way we think, in order to change the way we feel. We may feel angry enough to give someone the silent treatment or speak only words of criticism but the truth is, that feeling will lead us nowhere if we act on it. In the long run, it will fill us with contempt, dislike, defensiveness and resentment. I wish more of us would deliberately choose truth and life in our decisions, instead of instinctively following our feelings all the time. But as humans we are famous for following our feelings, aren't we?

The shame, blame and guilt game were corroding her like a slow growing moss on a tree in the forest. She was ashamed of her failing marriage, and blaming herself for feeling so fearfully responsible for the whole mess. Regret after regret was giving way to major guilt. They say to live in fear is to not live at all and I really do believe that.

Although I do bask in the idea of a love that keeps no record of wrongs, their scorecard was full. I believe they had no idea where they were headed.

Sometimes we trick ourselves into thinking we can continue the same behavior and get different results. Though the physical prison bars were not yet on the horizon, the mental and emotional stonewalls were being built slowly but surely around each of them.

The real jail cell was right around the corner, but who knew? It all looked so good from the outside. They lived the pretty, perfect and polished life with the dining room lights always on. Ostentatious suburbia at its best folks.

Bridgett kept her secrets safe; she hid her pain well and hobbled through her marriage without confronting or sharing the truth or extent of the emotional abuse with anyone in her family or even myself. Bridgett...well...she was like a chameleon, able to blend into whatever environment she found herself. I guess we all pretend in some way or another that we are bigger than our own secrets, but those secrets may have the power to conquer us if we don't take caution and heed wisdom. Yes, even our own hearts will deceive us if we are not careful. But of course, if no one knows, they may still think we are living the picture perfect life, right? On the other hand if no one knows, how can a person receive help? The truth cannot set us free until we are willing to face the lies. I suppose telling our secrets would cause us to fear what others may think, or perhaps we cannot stand the condescending judgment we may receive—from our family, our church, our neighbors and so called friends.

I remember the phone conversation with Bridgett when she finally started to open up to me about her life. It was as if the insidious floodgates had opened, the damn had collapsed. She rattled off a litany that has often come back to haunt me: "He (referring to her husband) checks my mileage, I am rarely allowed to open the mail. I must not answer the phone, we always let the machine pick it up, or he answers it. I don't call anyone for fear he will see the phone number on the bill. He goes away on business not telling me where, how I can reach him or even when he is coming back. If one of the twins got hurt…I just don't know what I would do. He has turned all the neighbors that I used to babysit for, against me, I have no friends." And on and on she went. The one that really got me was "I am on a two dollar a day budget." Put that together with suburbia and three kids and see what you come up with. After many long years of holding it in, raising twins and a baby practically as a single parent, the cloud over her situation came spewing out of her mouth like a tsunami that could not be held back any longer. Of course to be fair, this is only one side of a two-sided relationship. Still, I wish it wouldn't have taken her so long to expose it or for me to discover it. Early detection of these cautionary behaviors could save a person from a lifetime of misery. If your heart is beating out of its socket right about now, you may want to take a closer look at your own situation without fear involved. Fear kills any courage you may need to get out alive.

There is a lot more to the story, but I do know that she could count the days on one hand that they actually went on a date during their fifteen years of marriage. Babysitters were not an option, and ironically, their children rarely knew another caretaker. I don't know if it was: A. fear of someone else's influence on the children, B. paranoia or C. a sick motivation to keep Bridgett isolated. I am thinking it was "D" all of the above.

Bridgett was able to blend in perfectly no matter what her surroundings; many times expected to be nothing more than arm candy, a pretty trophy wife at church, or a sporting event. She became a pro at telling people what they wanted to hear just to keep the peace, avoiding confrontation at all costs.

She had played the perfect suburban housewife too long, and now had become the desperate housewife. Her story brings reality to desperation. Her life was now more parallel to the popular sit-com, Desperate Housewives, seen on television; than it ever had been before. The time had come; her desperation needed relief. So, to ease her pain she began drinking privately and often. Eventually, even this became unmanageable. Her pain was too deep, her loneliness and hurt were overwhelming and so was her drinking. The band-aid of a few beers or glasses of wine would no longer work, she moved on to drinking straight Vodka right out of the bottle. The bleeding had hemorrhaged. I believe she was drinking fast and furiously because this was the one way she could feel free from the box she was captive to, yet still living in. Maybe she thought her drinking was a way of regaining control of her life. I don't know. It was another secret on top of the thousands of others that I didn't know about for way too long. No matter which way I agonized trying to put the puzzle pieces together, they just never seemed to fit.

Granted, all Bridgett ever wanted was to love and to be loved back, which meant her and her husband would both need a heart full of forgiveness. Forgiveness comes harder for some than others, but un-forgiveness and resentment always put us in a prison of our own making regardless of the circumstances. Would she forgive him when he took his anger and stress out on her with the emotional abuse of name-calling and long periods of silence? Would he forgive her drinking, even though he himself drank as well? The fact that she started in AA proved she was beginning to take responsibility for her actions, but reconciliation always takes two people.

It is hard for people on the outside of a situation such as my friend's, to understand how someone can get so emotionally paralyzed through an abusive relationship and not get out of it. Why do people do this to themselves? I guess I can answer my own question here: because they feel trapped, they feel unworthy of a better life, they believe no one else would want them, or because the lies have brainwashed them to the point of full captivity. Many of us have been there- just on different levels. It could actually be happening to the woman next door to you. We should look closer into people's hearts rather than believing the masks they are wearing and try to help them out of the pit they are in through love, mercy and honest encouragement. It reminds me a lot of the woman at the well story in the Bible if you have ever heard of her.

Ironically, what neither my friend nor her husband understood was that the devil was getting exactly what he wanted. He comes to divide marriages, separate families and ruin relationships and He does it by lying and stealing dignity. If husbands and wives understood that our battle is not against each other, or flesh and blood, I wonder what our world would look like... if we quit expecting perfection and offered forgiveness? To reiterate, we must change the way we think, to change the way we feel.

The fairy tale ends here: where the failure to forgive begins.

SUBURBAN COMBAT

We seldom find victory over anything in our lives by avoidance.

The phone rang and the voice on the other end explained to me that Bridgett was in the hospital. There had been a terrible, terrible car accident. However, the name of the hospital was omitted from the conversation. "I'll pray," I thought to myself. "And God will answer," I hoped. "God, I need to know where my friend is," I whispered silently. I called information, while my heart was pounding out of my chest and told them the situation, "My best friend has been in a life-threatening accident, and I don't know what hospital she is in, but I have heard most accidents happen close to home." The operator gave me five hospitals close to her home. I was hoping it really did happen close to her home, because there are a lot of hospitals in Chicago. I picked up the phone again, tears rolling down my cheeks and dialed the first number on my list. "Do you have a

Bridgett --------, listed there?" "I will put you right through," the voice on the other end responded. God had answered, and answered now!

It was not only terrible but also more tragic than any of us anticipated. Another DUI, her third or fourth, (I had lost count) but this time she wrapped her car around a cement median and hit a man in the process. The man was in and out of the hospital within an hour, but Bridgett was not. She had fifty staples put in her head right on the hairline, her face now bloodied and bruised. Her ankle swelled up like a basketball, had been broken, cracked and fractured in five spots. Several vertebra in her back were fractured. After several operations, she ended up with pins in her ankle, which meant a special shoe cast, not to mention having to wear a back brace and some headgear too. As you can imagine, she was pretty much incapacitated, with a felony on her record to boot.

To make matters worse, her husband hand-delivered the newspaper article to her that sported her picture right along with the media side of the story on the front page of their local paper telling all about her accident, making a poster girl out of her. The public exposure of her downfall had to be difficult for him to swallow, to say the least, given his preoccupation with pretense. What would the neighbors think? Well, I'll answer that question: most of them thought whatever they were told. Why are we so quick to believe the bad news without all the facts? Many people tend to be surface or media junkies. Unfortunately, her accident was the straw that broke this camel's back; he went on to have her served with divorce papers while she was in the hospital as well. Are you getting the picture? I guess she no longer fit the mold of cover girl, her cover was blown. (Pun intended.) Please understand I am in NO way a fan of drunk drivers. I am just drawing a picture here for you from an eagle-eyed view of the best friend.

Even in the midst of the unfolding nightmare, I could see God at work. My husband had a conference preplanned the same week of Bridgett's car accident in the same city where she was hospitalized. As a matter of fact, he got to the hospital right after her husband had delivered the newspaper which was like rubbing salt in her wounds (as if she wasn't hurting enough.) They probably passed each other in the hall. God's timing was impeccable, much better than her husbands. God sent my husband as His helper to comfort her after not only the first blow of the car accident but after the second blow from the man who was supposed to love her for better or for worse. Could it have been that God was hoping that maybe her husband's heart would soften, and just maybe...she wouldn't be treated like a leper with some horrible disease, but rather a person, a hurting woman who needed one thing plain and simple: love in the form of forgiveness and some quality time, conversation and respect? Surely one would hope that by seeing his wife so humiliated, broken, and hopeless, he would come to see things differently.

When she finally came home there was hell to pay for the appearance of perfection had been blown all to hell in tiny little pieces. Now, can you imagine being cared for by the hands of an angry man who had just filed for divorce? She might have well been invisible. Bridgett's battle had just taken another deadly turn. I truly don't know which was worse, the hospital or the house. Under the circumstances, she wasn't allowed to leave the state. She was again isolated from family and she had no friends.

After her home combat sessions, she went into a 30-day rehabilitation treatment center, but not before a long drawn out insurance battle. For some odd reason, she was no longer on her husband's insurance plan? DUH! Eventually, the truth came out, and the man who had answered the phone when her husband called to remove her name from their insurance policy, (even though they were still married,) fessed up, told what happened and it is history from there. The truth always comes out one way or another. Bridgett got her insurance coverage back.

After her rehab, she went into a halfway house for more treatment, as she knew she could not go back home without drinking. She also knew she had to get her own life together in order to be the mother she had been to her boys at one time. Finally, she was ready to move forward with honesty and openness. She hadn't had a drink in months by this time but was still experiencing many physical, emotional, spiritual, and relationship sufferings.

After she had begun pulling herself out of the pit, and began healing from the accident she was told by her attorney that the courts had just ruled she'd spend 22 days in the county jail for her DUI.

Bridgett had once said to me, "Deb, I have turned my life over to the care of God and I will go wherever He calls me, just as long as that place is not jail." She then told me with a giggle, she knew that once she put that condition on it that she was sure she had sealed her fate. Be wary now, you are about to enter what was possibly one of the worst jails in the United States at the time of Bridgett's diary. We are now entering 22 Days in the County Jail with my bestest buddy in the whole world, my friend and confidant, Bridgett.

22 DAYS IN THE COUNTY JAIL

Bridgett's Journal

Wednesday, May 15, Day One

I get dressed in my "going to jail" outfit; a light gray, short sleeved, Tommy Hilfiger sweatshirt and black sweatpants--with my always spotless, white Keds. I also threw on a bright yellow Tommy Hilfiger long sleeved sweatshirt over my outfit as my roommate had told me how cold it is in jail. When I woke up in the morning I couldn't help but thank God for all my blessings; a beautiful, sunny day, three adorable, healthy boys, a supportive, caring family, a sensitive, loving male friend, wonderful, joyous roommates, and mostly a strong faith that God is keeping me in the palm of His hand. In preparing for jail, I have paid my bills, and got cards ready for my boys that my roommate will send every few days so they'll have some contact with me as I'm not sure if I'll be able to call them. I've memorized my phone card number and everyone's phone number I might want to call. I've packed an overnight bag for my Mom to give Deb for when she picks me up. I called Deb this morning for my morning spiritual pick me up but she wasn't' home. She told me she was going to fast from food while I'm in jail so that I would know when I am hungry I am not going through this alone.

I don't want long good-byes at this point, as I don't want to fall apart. I feel a great need to be strong and together at this point-more for the people around me. But, I say goodbye to my male friend, and totally fall apart. Why is it I always let my guard down around men? We say a quick good-bye and he leaves before he has a chance to fall apart. I hear him in the kitchen telling the girls from the halfway house to take care of me. How sweet, but unnecessary. They come into my bedroom and I explain everything that has transpired and how I am not moving my things out, I will be coming back to them. I pray that God will keep them from relapsing until I get back. As I am leaving, my other roommate, Sue, yells down the hall, "We'll be there tomorrow at noon for visiting hours- you can't shake us that easily." She is always so funny.

Now on to jail. I stay out with my parents, ending with a large lunch, until 3:30 p.m. I have to report to jail by 4:00 p.m. We finally found where to enter; my mom gets the phone number and address. I say my good-byes to my Dad out in the parking lot and my mom in the entrance. It had to be quick. I had to turn my back on my mom, as I can't stand to see the hurt she is feeling and to know that I caused it. I wish someday I'll be a daughter, mother, sister and wife to be proud of, but right now I don't think I could feel any lower. The walk down the long ramp is difficult. It's a beautiful, sunny, spring day, and it enters my mind that I could call my male friend and he would pick me up and we would go to Mexico and live happily ever after. Just a nice thought but I don't stop walking. I feel the sun on my face and God's presence is with me. I am not afraid, just anxious to get it over with, and a little apprehensive about what is going to happen in the next few hours. Nothing in my life has prepared me for this experience and I'm feeling quite vulnerable.

Ringing the bell to be let in the County Jail, I have in my possession, my clothes, my legal paperwork and $100.00 my dad gave me. The man on the other side of the speaker says, "Hello." I say, "I'm here to turn myself in." He tells me to "wait." Wait? What is this man thinking? This is not a good time to tell someone to wait. So I sit down on the step and sun my face. About ten minutes later he lets me in and asks if I'm bonding someone out. "No," I say, "I'm actually trying to get in!" The officer says, "Get in to see who?" "I'm not trying to see anyone, I'm trying to check myself in!" I say as if I'm checking myself into the classy hotels I'm accustomed to! The guard looks at my paperwork and I can see a light comes on in his head-his surprised look says- she's going to be an inmate-well I've seen everything now. A female guard lets me in and gently pats me down. "How many days you got?" asks the female guard, with long, black hair and petite yet very sturdy frame. "22" I respond. "I see you're in for aggravated DUI, a class four felony. Huh. You must have a really good lawyer." "Yes, I do," I say while thinking she really looks a lot like Cher, from Sonny and Cher. I tell her who my lawyer is and she says, "Oh, yeah, he's one of the best." She asks me to take off my yellow sweatshirt-telling me it's really not a good idea to be wearing two Tommy Hilfiger shirts to jail! She puts me in the holding cell right across from the guard's office. I'm beginning to notice that the guards are stopping by just to get a little look-see at the new jailbait. I am sure they are just checking out my freshly dyed, cut and styled platinum blonde hair.

Now there are a group of guards discussing where to put me-they've realized by now through some brief discussions with me, that I am a rich, suburban, stay at home mom, who has never been to jail, a dilemma to be sure. The one and only female officer says she does not think I'll be safe with the population as "they have a whole lot of scum right now." They all agree that I should go to segregation, a cell by myself I take it. They are using the wrap on my ankle as the excuse. A young, husky, bald male officer drops by for a viewing, "who's the doe caught in the headlights?" The enlarging group of officers laughs. "Just look at those eyes-she's scared to death!" He shot my hopes down. I thought I was looking so tough and secure. Yeah, right-who am I fooling? The inmates are now yelling down the hall wanting to know what's going on. Why are there so many guards? That's the gist of what they were saying in between expletives and profanity. The decision was made: I would call Seg Cell C my new home. The guard now unlocks my cell, "Come on Blondie, and let's go get you a new wardrobe." The inmates hear her and now know they have a blonde, white girl who is getting special attention.

Not a great predicament for me to be in! The name Blondie sticks and is usually yelled with some sort of profanity along with it. Off we go to change.

This was the part I have been dreading in my mind. At this point nothing, short of rape, would have surprised me. She points to a box of shower shoes and tells me to pick a pair. I'm obviously taking too long by the guard's reaction but they are all left shoes. I find the one and only right shoe which does not match the color of the left shoe. This bothers me immensely, of course being the color-coordinating queen that I am. She tells me to strip naked-oh God, here we go. I strip, putting my clothes in the paper bag she has provided. She has me open my mouth. I guess she's checking out my recently bleached teeth? "Shake out your hair." I must have a stupid look on my face, as she shows me how to do it. I shake my hair. Maybe she's checking for roots? You won't see any on my head. Three weeks from now that'll be a different story. She asks me now to turn around, squat and cough. I indignantly ask her, "You want me to do what?" "Oh forget it and get in the shower, here's your clothes and your towel. Come to the guards station when you are done." That was not so bad now was it, I thought? Then I looked at the nightmare they called a shower. There is no way you could come out of that mold and scum infested cube--cleaner than you went in. I opted only to put my arm in the shower. How many days could I go without showering before I can't stand my own smell I wondered? I start to get dressed in my 44 DD light pink stretch bra. It's not wonderfully uplifting considering I am a 34B. I'm really missing my wonder bra about now. I put on underpants that reach up to my ribcage. Next come my T-shirt and matching bright orange pants that are so large they could wrap around my size 4 figure twice. I have to hold the pants up with one hand when I walk. The guard thinks it's pretty funny. I have learned one thing; orange does not become me. I have truly been humbled. Maybe this is why God sent me here.

Thursday, May 16, Day Two

I wake up in the cell-the room with a view. I have a window from floor to ceiling and about 6 feet wide. I can see the sky, grass, some birds and a really ugly cement wall. I wake up and thank God for giving me this day. I ask God to watch over, protect and bless my children. I ask the Holy Spirit to pray for me today as I am having a hard time praying right now. The words are just not there. I never leave my cell today. I do not see or talk to another inmate. One very kind officer comes down to talk to me. I'm at the end of a very long, skinny hallway that no one comes down without a reason. The officers do come down every half-hour to make sure I'm still alive but rarely say anything. Officer Barton is a white male, 6 foot 4 inches, in very good shape. He smiles a lot and has kind eyes that look very sad even though he's smiling. He is a breath of fresh air-he brings me some books - Dr. Phil's Life Strategies, a romance novel, and some paper and 2 pencils. It is so kind of him especially since he could get in trouble for this. He also gets me a pillow since I don't have one. He tells me pretty much his life story. His days running the streets in a gang, his service in the armed forces, his seven years working here at the jail and how he either wants to be a U.S. Marshall or a full time private body guard. I guess he needed to talk as much as I needed to listen.

I am going to be in solitary confinement until at least next Wednesday. That's the only day the doctor comes in. I really wouldn't mind this so much, but I cannot stand the coldness. My cell is freezing and they will only give me one thin blanket. I wear both sets of my clothes and I sleep with my arms pulled inside my tee shirt. I am shivering all the time and my hands are so cold I can hardly write this journal. I'm naturally a cold person but never like this. I'll never take my warm home for granted again. Maybe this is why God sent me here.

Friday, May 17, Day Three

I wake up thanking God for a new day. I ask His protection and care for my children. This is a tough morning. I am sobbing as I think about my children getting ready for school without their mom. They have suffered so much because of my addiction. I know their dad is doing his best, taking care of their basic needs, but he has never been one to understand emotional needs. That's what my kids need their mother for and I won't be able to be there for them for quite a while. I pray that when I can be part of their lives again that the distance between us will not be too great to be overcome. I'm looking forward to giving my children a healthy mother that they can be proud of. That is my guiding light. It drives me on to do the right thing day by day; sometimes it's hour by hour that I fight my addiction. My addiction is rearing its lovely ears today. A drink would only make my problems worse, if that's possible, but it would certainly help me escape the here and right now.

Maybe reading will help me get out of this mindset. There are six things I can do to bide my time: sleep, read, write, pray, exercise and daydream. Writing seems to be the most time consuming as I can write this journal, start a book, write my fourth step, or write letters. I have to stop writing now to get under covers and try to get warm. This day has been extremely long. I cannot see a clock so I only can kind of tell what time it is by when the meals come. I can hear the TV blaring all day long, but I can't see it and I can hear the girls talking and singing and fighting but I can't see them. Where I am at is supposed to be a punishment cell. I now know why the guards keep asking me what I did to get myself in here. The guards are actually quite helpful if you are respectful to them. They seem to be tolerant of the prisoners to a point-but do not swear at or call a guard a name or you will be in one of these cells like mine-only with no window, no sheets, no pillows, no books and you'll be lucky if they let you have your clothes! I now know I possess the inner strength and courage to get through this or anything else they throw my way! Maybe this is why God sent me here.

Saturday, May 18, Day Four

Another freezing night. My hips and shoulders are beginning to get bruised, as the mat they call a bed is rock hard. My muscles are very stiff and my ankle really needs a walk to loosen it up. I limp like I am 90 years old over to get my breakfast - this cheers me right up - a bug infested donut, and a glass of milk. I don't know what the brown lumpy stuff is they serve every morning. I don't plan on ever taste testing it either. Maybe I'll do some sit-ups to warm up.

About 1:30 they yell at me to get my things together. I am moving. They have a suicide attempt to put in my room. They come in a yellow blanket, naked, with no sheets, no pillow, and just a plastic mat. What a way to live. To get to my new cell, the guard keys open one gate, we go through a small area they call the catwalk, electronically another barred gate slides open. I am now in a room with eight women, who have stopped playing cards, drawing and watching TV to stare blatantly. A blue-eyed blonde definitely stands out in this crowd. Another gate is keyed open, this is my cell. I meet my roommate, Karen. She is a heavy set woman in her late forty's with thick black layered hair, with a heavy gray streak right through the front. I am now in the middle of maximum security. My situation just keeps getting better and better. My bunk is five feet off the ground. Karen yells at the guard asking her "How is this woman supposed to get up there with a broken ankle?" "She can sleep on the ground for all I care." So much for the kind guards. I get my mat, pillow, and sheets up on the top bunk. I soon realize it is easy to get up on my bunk but hopping off with a broken foot is not so easy. I am very apprehensive about my roommate but she soon puts me more at ease. She has very kind blue eyes. She is soon showing me the ropes. Again, I will not be allowed out except for showers. Everything in here is bars. This is a cage within a cage within a cage. I really feel this is an inhumane way to live - even if you need to be in maximum security - but for a DUI, this is way too much. Karen is in here for medical reasons too, but she has been sentenced to ten years.

She'll be here for another week and a half, finishing her time for drug possession and intent to sell, then she is going on to a penitentiary for a few years, for I don't know what. That's what scares me. She has a broken hand right now from an altercation with another prisoner. I think I'll just stay up here on my perch and write and be quiet. The women out in maximum security sleep on the floor on mats at night from 10 p.m. to 6 a.m. The rest of the day they mill about the middle cage together, talking, watching TV, reading, and drawing. They can shower and make phone calls anytime they want. The women in maximum-security are a very diverse group. They knew my whole story within ten minutes of my arrival. There are two very tall, large, intimidating white girls who look like twins and they rarely speak. There is one very sweet, very pregnant Mexican looking girl, Marybeth, who draws all the time. She is 21 years old and eight months pregnant with her seventh child! She has had a baby every year since she was 14. She claims she was on birth control and this is her first time in jail. She will be delivering her baby at the nearby hospital and will have 24 hours with her baby, then back to prison. Her boyfriend is supposed to come and get the baby. She will have three more months to serve after the delivery. There is another Mexican girl named Carry, with beautiful long, black hair, and a very warming smile, and a word of some kind tattooed on her ankle and back. Her nickname is "40" because she likes to drink 40 ounce malt liquors. She is very talkative. She was only out of jail for four hours, she drank three 40 ouncers and climbed in a window of a house with a man in it. She claims she was not there to rob him but doesn't really remember the incident. That's the problem with alcohol - those blackouts are terrible. She assaulted the police officer trying to arrest her and received another felony indictment for that and wound up right back in jail not remembering just what had occurred.

There are three large black women who harmonize together when they sing. Two of them are always talking at the same time and every other word is swearing; many of which I have never heard but get the gist of. One of them is very quiet and stares at me. I have the feeling she is waiting for me to say something to her so she can jump all over my case. She's going to be waiting a while because I'm not biting. Nikki is around 20, very smooth black skin, tiny curled braids, thickly lashed, warm, brown eyes and perfect white teeth (a rarity around here.) She has a smile that lights up the room and a great sense of humor. She seems to be the class clown among the inmates.

After dinner they let me out to take a shower. The shower is behind a wall but the phone and the toilet are also back there. There are maggots in the shower drain that are visible; the water comes out of an old shampoo bottle stuck on the showerhead. The floor is very slippery as the soap scum is thick and you have to hold the button in to get water. At least the water is warm. As soon as I get out of the shower and comb my hair the guard tells me I have a visitor. She says she looks like my sister. I enter the visitor's room and it has three cells with a stool and a phone, divided by a window. Sitting at the first station is my roommate, Sue, with a huge smile. It was so great to see her. We talk and laugh over the phones not working and in walks my male friend. What a beautiful sight! I've never been so glad to see anyone in my life. Once again I was so overwhelmed I was shaking. I had told him not to come, as I did not want him to see me like this. Out rears vanity's ugly head again. He told me I couldn't do that to him and he was coming anyway. The nerve of some men. So here he is and he looks so good. I think I'm finally realizing what unconditional love is from a man-it has nothing to do with his looks, but that doesn't hurt either! I definitely never had this with my husband. I only am realizing that now. I definitely feel as though my male friend could do a lot better. He does not deserve a girlfriend five years older than him, getting divorced, fighting a custody battle, a recovering alcoholic, and in jail. I really don't think in negative terms about my life too often, but let's get real. God has always blessed me with a positive attitude no matter what life throws at me. As for my male friend, well I am sure God has given me something to offer him that he needs. He obviously sees something in me that I don't. Maybe it's my unconditional love for him. He has slowly been opening up to me about his past and I do not judge him for anything he has done. I listen and I understand. In fact I admire him for being able to overcome such a difficult life. He has turned his life around to become a very caring, sensitive, open and passionate man. To be the recipient of his love is such a gift. God is so awesome.

Well, we visited and laughed a lot, as we always do, and I cried, of course. It's only been four days since I've seen them but it feels like ages. My male friend told me he's agreed to be Sue's temporary sponsor. It was a hard decision for her on what type of sponsor a gay female should have. A gay female was out of the question because there could be an attraction and a straight female might be uncomfortable, so a man it is. He will be very good for her if she listens to him. She definitely needs some good direction. She seemed like she was having a hard time.

Our time is up. I can only get one visit a week for 30 minutes. I stand up to leave and my male friend pretends to be checking me out, which makes me laugh! He actually told me I look good in 'orange'. Liar. I told him to "go through my closet and throw away any orange." " I wish you were wearing yellow," he replies. It took me a minute to get that. He's not fond of all the bright yellow that I wear. Black is his favorite color. I guess that explains it all. Sue and I throw kisses at one another backing out of the room.

"I never have that much fun on my visits," the inmate next to me exclaims. During my visit, Nikki from max was sitting two seats down from me visiting with her mother. She had gotten back to the cage before me and had filled all the girls in on who my visitors were. I entered the cage to catcalls and whistles, much to my supreme embarrassment. "We heard you got yourself one, big, sweet, white boy." "That's why she smiles all the time." "I'd do that man right..." and on and on they went for 15 minutes and it got cruder and cruder.

They let me stay out of my cell that night and watch TV. The girls braided each other's hair and talked very loudly all at the same time. One by one most of them came and sat next to me and they all seemed to want some kind of advice or maybe they just needed someone to listen to them without talking. They showed me how to make ponytail holders from the tops of socks, curlers out of toilet paper, tampons out of maxi pads and makeup out of colored pencils. They are quite resourceful. They also take maxi-pads and put them on the ceiling where it is leaking. This area is supposed to be condemned because of the leaks but they have never shut it down. When they shut the TV off at 10 p.m. I go back to my cell and the girls lay their mats down on the cold, wet cement floor right outside my cell. I cannot believe the inhumane conditions in this jail. They told me joke after joke and we laughed and laughed until about 1 a.m. Usually the guards don't let us talk after lights out but tonight they thought it was nice to hear everyone laughing. The guard later told me that was the first night they'd had in weeks without a fight. God was working the late shift again! Maybe this was why God sent me here.

Sunday, May 19, Day Five

When we woke up, the girls were told to pack up. They were being split up into different dormitories. It took a couple hours for them to actually do the change. I thanked them for the great slumber party the night before. I had not laughed that hard in a long time. It's so quiet in here now, but it's nice not to have that constant, loud chatter. No one here seems to know how to talk, they all yell at one another to be heard. Now the only sound is the TV and the girl, Lynn, two cells down who has been in jails and mental institutions since she was ten years old. She's a young, black woman in her early 20's, with thick glasses and weighs about 300 pounds. She's extremely violent and I was told she had recently punched a bunch of officers here. It took a total of eight officers with pepper spray to subdue her.

She tried unsuccessfully to hang herself in her cell a couple of days ago and is always trying to hurt herself. I sat next to her last night when I was watching TV, the cell bars were between us but she could've reached out and grabbed me anytime she wanted. She talked to me like she was a sweet little child. I feel very sorry for her and what life holds for her. I've prayed and asked for the angels that Deb asked to watch over me and keep me warm, to watch over her instead. She needs them more than I do.

Today is a very hard day for me as I am missing my visitation with the boys. My heart just aches for what I am putting them through. I've cried many tears today for them. All I can do for them now is keep going down the right path and try my best to put together a good life for us.

Monday, May 20, Day Six

Karen and I are let out of our cells to clean the day room. I sweep the day room and she cleans the bathroom and shower. Using some cleaner and a maxi-pad as a rag, no pun intended. I clean the two tables in the room, as clean as you can get tables that have pealing, yellow paint with blue paint underneath. My sweeping job now has Karen complaining at me. She can do it herself if she does not like it. Of course, I don't have the gumption to tell her that. I was very depressed today and slept a lot.

Tuesday, May 21, Day Seven

I've made it a week. Only two more to go. I was up all night again; between the four of them snoring it sounds like I'm sleeping in a cave of bears. There's also Cindy's nightmares, Karen's talking in her sleep and then there's Vinnie. Vinnie is another story all together. Her cell is to the right of mine and I don't know her story except she's in segregation because she's a violent mental case. She sleeps all day and is up all night and talks to the guard when he comes in every half-hour. She weighs about 225 pounds and every time she sits on her bed, Karen and I are almost bounced off our bunks as they are on a connecting steel wall that shakes. She likes to rock herself to sleep, which in turn rocks us, which makes Karen scream at her.

I can tell I am beginning to lose energy from not eating and not moving. I've barely eaten anything since I've been here, but I really am not that hungry. Karen has been kind enough to share her commissaries with me. I really believe that they make the food so terrible so that the inmates will buy commissaries. What a racket. Commissaries are any type of toiletries like shampoo, conditioner, lotion, also paper goods like tablets, envelopes, stamps, pencils, and a variety of snacks. They are all reasonably priced. Tomorrow I will have been here eight days and it is the first time I will be receiving them. I'm looking forward to washing my hair. I went about twenty days after my car accident without washing my hair though. I could really use that deodorant. I smell quite repugnant now. I wash every morning, and shower every other day but when you live and sleep in the same clothes and don't use any deodorant there's not a whole lot you can do. We did get new pants today though. This was my first spat with my roommate. The officer came and exchanged our towels and asked what size pants we'd take. Karen told the guard that she would take a 3X and to get me a 1X and the guard started to walk away. I said, "Excuse me officer, I'll take a small." Karen yells over me, "F that, give her a large." "Karen I think I know what size I am better than you and I wear a small." The guard brings me a small and waits while I take off the pants I have on and hand them to him. I put on the small and they were rather big on me. She told me I'm getting snippy. I told her she's getting really bossy with me and the few decisions we have to make for ourselves in here I would like to make myself. She tells me I should be grateful that I have such a nice roommate and I agree with her that she has been very nice to me. She seems to be placated. Karen is going to court tomorrow to be sentenced to ten years in prison and she is getting more and more irritated and aggressive as the time gets closer. Anytime I am not pretending to be sleeping she wants to talk to me constantly, making it very hard to read or write. I've found it easier to just shake my head in agreement with her than say anything that might get her in an argument. She said she needs to get her badass attitude back before she goes to prison.

Karen asked me to cut her hair today before she goes to court and I agreed-not knowing that I have to use toenail clippers to do it. Her hair is very thick and curly. I cut about an inch off the top, layering the whole thing and trim the back, which is halfway down her back. She sat on the toilet while I cut it and she kept a look out for the guards, as we would get in serious trouble for doing this. The whole episode took about an hour, and I must say it looked marvelous. At least Karen was pleased, so I'm safe for another day.

She wrote me out her recipe for Italian sauce with sausage and meatballs as a thank you. I told her my male friend was Italian and I was never going to cook him pasta until his mother shows me how to make it. So she wrote it out step by step, six pages in all. It would take me all day to make this dinner but I'm anxious to try it out when I get home. Back to the halfway house or apartment… that is. I've been thinking a lot about where home should be when I'm finished with my 90 days at the halfway house. I'm really missing my kids right now and I want to live where all of us will be happy. It's tough also because I want my male friend to be a part of my life, and know I love him deeply, but he keeps saying he wants to go to Florida to live and I don't want to do anything to impede his happiness and I know I cannot go with him. For that reason, I didn't want to become too attached to him, but it's like I just can't help myself even though I have not known him very long.

It's so quiet tonight. If Cindy, Vinnie and Lynn all take their meds at dinner they go right to sleep afterwards. Karen sat here and told me stories of her days running with a motorcycle gang. The guard came and collected one of our t-shirts, our bras, and our socks to wash. We have two pair of underwear that we have to wash by hand in the sink.

This day has been long since we have not been let out of our cell since this morning. God grant me patience has been my prayer today. Maybe this is why God sent me here.

Wednesday, May 22, Day Eight

Vinnie kept us up all night again. I can't take being in this psycho ward anymore. I'm supposed to see the doctor today to get off of segregation. No matter what, I am determined to get out of this cellblock today. The breakfast, which they bring us at 5:30 a.m., consists of biscuits with gravy, sausage and oatmeal. I don't eat breakfast so the other girls share mine. They really don't need an extra helping as they are all way overweight. Karen said she has gained 50 pounds in this County Jail. The girls all think they have great bodies and are very sexy. It makes me envious of their attitude toward themselves, as I have never viewed my body as sexy. In fact I've always been extremely self-conscious about my body. I warned my male friend from the beginning, that his grandmother probably has a better-looking stomach than I do because of my twin pregnancy. The first thing he said was, "Well, let me see it and I'll be the judge." Suffice it to say; by his reaction it never bothered him. I've been doing 300 sit-ups, leg lifts, push-ups, and a few other exercises every day since I've been here. I'm trying not to totally lose what little muscle tone I have and to keep my energy up, which seems to be draining. I find myself having less energy every day and I'm sleeping more and more during the day. I am definitely losing my concentration to write every day. Motivation comes and goes. I'm trying to stay focused.

Karen is going to court this morning and Vinnie is going to video court. Karen is so nervous. She is being sentenced to ten years in the Penitentiary and she is actually happy about it. She says she'll only have to do four years of it. According to Karen prison is a lot better than jail. They make jail so horrible so that you never want to come back. Karen has already done a four and half year stint at the

Pen. A lot of good that did. I asked her if she is going back to the same old life when she gets out. "Hell yes, four years is just a hitch in my step." "I'll be partying till I die." Some people just view prison as a different way of life, not as a punishment.

The guard was not in a good mood and would not tell Karen if she was on the court list. She got very upset; yelling at him and calling him a list of every name she could think of. He just walked away. He finally came back and very smugly told her that she was on the list and yes she could take a shower. She put makeup on and fussed over her hair and clothes like she was going on a date. She kept remarking how beautiful her hair is. Which I agreed with her and how any woman would kill to have her curls. Whether or not she should wear one or two tee shirts was of great concern to her. Like it really matters, they're both bright orange! She opts for two over her thermals, as it might be cold in the courthouse. It is really hard to see in this light how her makeup looks but I reassure her again and again that she looks quite beautiful. She tells me that the male inmates always whistle at her and she knows a couple of the guards have crushes on her. This amuses me to no end! She finally gets let out to get her shackles on. Her hands will be handcuffed to a chain that goes around her waist for the rest of the day. She will have to eat and go to the bathroom this way. I can't imagine how she will manage that, but then that is something I don't really want to imagine! Before she leaves she tells me that she feels God sent me to her so that she could take care of me. I just smile and nod my head. I find myself doing that quite often lately.

With Karen and Vinnie gone, I am grateful that no one has turned on the televisions. I lie down and take a wonderfully quiet nap until lunchtime.

I finally got to see the doctor this afternoon. He's a very kind old man in his 70's. I tell him and the nurse that I have been in segregation since I got here eight days ago. He cannot believe that they did that to me. He looks at my foot and we talk about my neck and what has transpired since the accident. He calls the Sergeant and complains about how I have been treated and orders me into general population. The guard walking me back, a very attractive Mexican man, suddenly turns his attitude toward me from hostile to quite sympathetic. Most of the people in seg are there because they are violent and he must have thought it was my story too. He asks me what is wrong, and tells me I can stay out in the dayroom for a while, where I have a very pleasant conversation with Lynn. When I get back to my cell I'm very apprehensive about joining general population. Fear of the unknown. I open my Bible for comfort and it falls open to Matthew. "Therefore, I tell you, do not worry about tomorrow, for tomorrow will worry about itself. Each day has enough trouble of its own. (Matthew 6:34 NIV)

Karen returns from court and is really pissed off that she did not get sentenced. She has a new court date in June sometime. She has an officer from another prison she's supposed to go to after the Penitentiary and they want to roll the two sentences together into one. She may get pissed off but once she swears it out of her system she calms down easily. She wanted to know if the doctor signed the paper to get her out of seg and I explained that the nurse said she had her covered, whatever that means. She wanted to know all about what the doc said about my foot. She's all worried about me keeping the wrap off and my foot swelling too big. She's so caring and such a mother hen. The guard came by and told us we've been approved; to pack up we'll both be moving. Karen tells the guard we want to go to the dorm and the guard says he'll tell her what she can do. We start to pack and Karen begins her instructions on what I need to know.

Basically, she instructs me that I'll walk in behind her, she'll scope out where her group of friends are and we'll lay our mats out there. She says once everyone knows I'm with her, I'll be left alone. She tells me "Walk in there strong," then she looks me up and down, and says, "Well, just give it a try will ya."

We are ready to go, not knowing we have another three hours before we move. Our mail comes and I have two letters from Deb, one from Sue and one from my parents. Karen and I sit on her bed and read them together. They are all so loving and supportive that I can't help but cry. With such wonderful support carrying me, how can I fail? I'm destined for success. The cards have made me really homesick. I desperately want to go home. I can't help but think about how fortunate I am to have the halfway house as my home. I have wonderful roommates and a nice apartment to call home. I can't sit here and feel sorry for myself that I'm not at home with my kids. I have created this life passage and I am responsible and accountable for where I am in my life. Where I am at, what I am experiencing and where I go from here is a direct result of the choices I have and will make. I realize now how my choices directly affect all of those around me, especially my kids. I'm fighting for their lives right now.

This experience has humbled me and made me realize how fortunate I am. Lynn cries constantly that she wants to go home. Her home is a Mental Health Facility. She's been living there on and off since she was ten. She's now 26 and calls that home. Cindy, who rarely speaks, also complains that she wants to go home. She's here because she got drunk and rolled over on her newborn baby in bed and smothered him to death. Her mind has taken her to a place where she does not remember what she has done or why she is locked up. She just says she knows she did something really, really bad. She cries at night that she wants to go home to her baby and sings, "Rock a Bye Baby" all the time. My heart just breaks for these women. How could I ever feel bad about going home to a halfway house?

Well, we're finally moving to the dorm. When we walk in the door, it's just as Karen says. Everyone starts yelling at me and telling me where to lay my mat. Karen points to a spot and tells me there. Everyone yells at me, "You don't have to listen to her." I do listen of course. She has not let me down so far. She knows the ropes; she's kind, tough and lucky for me--straight!

The floor is now where I call home. I wedged between three bunks and all the women are named Betty. Go figure that one. This seems to be the social corner of the dorm. It houses 24 women. 10 on the floor and 14 on bunks. We're all in one huge room with four tables in the middle, one TV, two sinks but only one works. Two toilets, two showers and absolutely no privacy. Betty, to my left, quickly befriends me, and begins the tale of her lifelong cocaine addiction. After about two hours I've talked her into receiving treatment when she leaves jail. I'm going to send her some info through the mail on treatment centers that accept women with no medical insurance. I'll also send her some stamped envelopes so she can write to those places and get on their waiting list. She's so grateful she's almost in tears. Maybe this is why God sent me here.

I'm really tired so I move my mat to a quieter area where the girls are sleeping. It's a long while before sleep comes though.

Thursday, May 23, Day Nine

Sleeping on the floor is just as bad as it sounds. If the hair and the dirt don't disgust you, the bugs surely will. My mat is by the trashcan so the fruit flies are a nuisance but I can't really see any place else neutral to move. I don't eat breakfast so the girls are all vying for my tray. I can see this is going to be a problem. The doctor was kind enough to prescribe me some Motrin for inflammation of my ankle. He didn't take my ace bandage though so I'm going to put it back on. After breakfast and meds most of the girls go back to sleep. I use this chance to shower when they're not all around. I know it's going to be hard to journal during the day with these people talking to me so morning will be a good time for that too.

Everyone in the dorm appears to get along pretty well. If they don't, they're controlling themselves very well. I'm quite surprised actually. Time will tell though. The biggest problem I can see with the dorm is the officers do not check on it, and do not seem to want to help anyone with anything. The girls in here don't get their commissary and they are charged for it, can't get new clothes when they fall apart, don't even get to see the doctor or the social worker. It's like they put you in this room, lock the door and forget about you. This is supposed to be the sanest room in the whole jail though.

Most of the women read the Bible and do daily devotionals. They all seem to be interested in my views on God and the Bible. I asked Betty why she was so interested in my opinion. She said, "Blondie, you are so positive and you always have a smile on your face. I just want to know how you do it." I still believe God is with me every step of the way and I am here for a reason.

The girls all want to know why I am writing so much and I am afraid someone will try to read this. That might make life very difficult for me, as I have been brutally honest in this journal. If I lose Karen's support, I could be in trouble.

My day is spent much the same, reading, writing, and sleeping only with more talking in between. After dinner I have begun to feel really sick to my stomach and the room is spinning. I don't even think I could stand up and walk without falling. I don't know if it's because I haven't eaten right, or the inner ear problem caused by my accident. I laid down while it was still light out and just retreated to my own mind till morning.

Friday, May 24, Day Ten

The nights here are always rough. One very young heroin addict was throwing up all night. I felt very sorry for her but there's not much I can do to help her. It doesn't seem to faze anyone else. I guess they are used to it. I'm still dizzy, but it's not as bad when I'm sitting up.

There is definitely a routine you must follow here. The lights come on at 5 a.m. Breakfast comes at 5:30 a.m. Then we lay back down till meds and cleaning supplies come. Then I have to pick up all my stuff and put it on the table so that they can clean the floors. Then we lay back down until about 10 a.m. Sleeping late makes the days go by much faster. Things stay pretty quiet around here until around dinner. Then people become very social and tempers begin to flare. No one ever leaves this dorm unless they are going to court. No one has a job and most people are waiting to be bonded out. I lay next to Tammy's bunk. She is a very tough white woman, 22, with reddish, almost orange hair. She's very social if she likes you. She has two children, boys, ages three and four years and a boyfriend. She wants to marry her boyfriend this summer but he is in prison right now. She wants a storybook wedding gown and the works. Only her storybook has a twist, she actually wants to be six or seven months pregnant when she walks down the aisle! When I inquire why she thinks this would be a good thing, she explains she looks her best when she's pregnant. Her skin clears up and she looks pregnant instead of fat! Another time when I just nod and shake my head. She begins to tell me her story. She does not do drugs and she rarely drinks but she was arrested for being in a car that was selling drugs to an undercover policeman. She steers clear of drugs and alcohol because she was raised by an alcoholic mother, who totally neglected her and her three brothers. They were left to fend for themselves from a very early age. Tammy is now sobbing on my shoulder and everyone in the dorm is now staring at us. This woman never lets her guard down. At the young age of ten she had had enough of her mother's way of life. She begged her mother to go to AA and Tammy took her mother to her first meeting! Her mom has now been clean and sober for 12 years and is active in AA sponsoring people and has chosen counseling addicts for her career. Tammy's mom is now taking care of her children and is going to bond her out on Tuesday. What a great testimonial on what the power of a daughter's love and the fellowship of AA can do in a person's life. It's a powerful combination that only the hand of God could create.

A new girl comes into the dorm looking quite bewildered as to where to lay her mat. Tammy shows her around. She tells her "The wall with the old people is the retirement village. The wall with the Mexican girls is the projects. The wall with the white girls is the trailer trash area…. and this is Blondie--she's just slumming it." This was greeted with a roar of laughter! Yeah. Yeah. Very funny.

Saturday, May 25, Day Eleven

I'm half way there! I've been here 11 days. 11 to go. I actually can't believe it's only been 11 days. It feels like so much longer. I'm sure it will get easier the closer I get. At least I hope so. I think it's really hard here in the dorm because we can't see outside.

I finally got through to Deb. My spiritual guru and my only connection to the outside world. She has called my kids for me and left a message from me. She is definitely my voice when I have none. I know my calls to her are really expensive but she tells me not to worry. I think she knows how important our talks are to me. I told her that I'd be out of here June 5th in the morning. She told me she'll come up here the night before and she'll stay as long as I need her. How lucky, I am to have her for a friend.

Two of the girls in here Carry, (the girl who was out of jail for four hours and got arrested again) and Loretta, an older white lady with black hair and a very bad attitude, have asked me if I could find them a sponsor when I leave here. They will be going on to prison from here so all contact will have to be in writing. Carry has expressed several times a sincere desire to stop drinking. I feel she really means it. I told her that I would do my best to help her and that I would write her and send her AA info until I found her a sponsor. Maybe this is the reason God sent me here.

I find myself spending most of my time sitting on my mat reading, writing or exercising. I'm friendly with everyone but I don't make an effort to socialize too much. If people want to speak to me they come sit by me and they always seem to have a good reason for coming to me. I don't socialize because I'm not entertained by old war stories about prison, drugs and sex. I just don't want to get involved in that talk and it's too hard to get away once you're involved in the group. Avoidance is working for me at this point.

Officer Barton came to the dorm today. It was nice to see his smiling face. He always makes it a point to find me and say something encouraging. He's one of the few officers that really seem to care about the prisoners and treat them like real people. He asked me if I needed anything, and I told him the commissary sent me erasers instead of pencils. He's always encouraging me to keep writing. He comes back about 20 minutes later and calls me out of the dorm. Out in the hallway he gives me some pencils and tells me not to let the girls know. He could get reprimanded for doing favors for a prisoner. I express to him how grateful I am. I tell him I'm half way through my sentence and he puts out his bottom lip and says, "Who am I to bring pencils to?" "I'm sure you'll find someone." He laughs. "I don't think anyone else knows how to write!" It just dawns on me, this man is flirting with me - you don't have to hit me over the head with a rock do you!

I should be getting a visit tonight. I hope it's with my male friend, and one of my roommates - not just my roommates. I love my roommates but I've had enough of girl talk.

Time goes by so slowly when I'm waiting for a visit. I borrowed Karen's eyeliner/coloring pencil and Carry is showing me how to soak it and apply it. Carry always has her makeup on and her hair done. We now have everyone's input and this is becoming a major production. I must say, once it's applied, it doesn't look half-bad. Like I said, even jail isn't taking away my vanity! I'm not nearly as self-conscious as I used to be.

Just when I was beginning to think that no one was coming the guard calls me for my visit. The dorm I am in is right in the middle of the men's section, which I believe is why we never get to leave the dorm. There are 700 men here and about 80 women. I understand now that I am being paraded by the men to get to my visit. I am really dizzy as I am walking down the hall. This has been going on for four days now. As I sit down in the visiting room the whole room is spinning. I'm really nervous and I'm not sure why. In walks my male friend, I was so glad he was there. I don't know what I would do without him. He does not realize how important he is to me. He has such a positive outlook on life even when things aren't going his way. I'm very worried about him. His Mom, whom he dearly loves and is very close with, is having another surgery, he's not getting any hours at his job, and his new job won't start until he gets a week training in. I'm in jail and his sponsor is out of town. This is a very hard time for him and I wish I could be there for him. All I can do is call on God to protect him and keep him in the palm of His hand and have faith that my prayers will be answered. He has a very strong program going, much stronger than mine, but I still worry about him relapsing. Being alone is one of the worst feelings a person can have. I hope he realizes he's not alone. I'm always with him. Back to the visit: he tells me that I'm not alone and he puts his hand over his heart and pats it. He always gives me the nicest compliments telling me how strong and courageous I am - I think he's actually trying to convince me of that for my own benefit. He is definitely a man of great faith and it shows through in his speech and his actions. He gave me the scoop on everyone at the halfway house. I had so many questions I wanted to ask him and I forgot them all. My mind just went blank. I have a very hard time saying what I feel or what's troubling me. He says it's like pulling teeth getting me to say what's on my mind. The 30 minutes for our visit just is not long enough. It's really heartwarming to know that I have such a great person waiting for me. The visit ends unfortunately and I walk back to the dorm without any emotion at all. Sometimes I feel as though so much has happened to me that my emotions have been blunted.

On Saturday nights we get to watch a movie. The girls ask the guard for popcorn and coke but I don't think he's going to oblige them. The movie is called, "From Hell" and is about Jack the Ripper. It's something different to do anyway. I rarely watch TV here. My mat is right under the TV so I can't see it unless I move my lazy butt. Usually the talking is so loud you can't hear it anyway.

All in all it wasn't such a bad day. I spent a lot of time reading the Bible today. Maybe this is why God sent me here.

Sunday, May 26, Day Twelve

Sundays are just destined to be a depressing day for me. It really upsets me to miss my visitation with my little boys. I think this is my worse consequence because it not only hurts me but more so them.

I'm really in a bad mood today. I'm homesick, my whole body hurts from sleeping on the dirty, bug infested floor. I wouldn't feed this food to my dogs. I want out of this room so bad I could scream! But I put on my mask, as I am accustomed to doing. I smile and pretend that everything is just fine. Well it's not fine, it sucks. I'm tired of hearing disgusting stories, I'm sick of hearing how people are not guilty of their crimes, over and over again and pretending to be interested. I hate that my boys have a mother who is in jail, that I'm worrying my parents, that my male friend has to visit me here and see me like this. I'm sick of the women in here with a warped sense of right and wrong, who yell and cuss on one hand and quote the Bible while they're doing it. I'm having a hard time today, figuring out my mantra: why God sent me here - I don't think I really want to know right now.

We went to church services in the evening and the preacher was from a Baptist church. It was more of a quick Bible study than anything else. The preacher's theme though was quite appropriate - God has sent you here to jail for a reason - do you know why?

Monday, May 27, Memorial Day, Day Thirteen

This year is not starting out so well holiday wise. My birthday was spent at home, fresh out of the hospital with my husband and his mother, both treating me like dirt. They of course refused to leave my house and let my parents come until after my birthday was over. It was sheer torture. But then, that's what they intended it to be. Then came Easter, I spent it totally alone living at the halfway house. My roommates were all gone. My husband would not even discuss letting me see the kids and our court date for visitation wasn't until the next week. I tried to call the kids but to no avail of course. I did talk to my family on the phone that day and my male friend called me from his family party but it was very lonely. I didn't even get to church because I had no one to drive me. I slept most of the day.

Well, aren't my holidays getting better and better? Memorial Day in jail. They could not figure out how to turn the lights on in the dorm this morning. Since there are no outside lights, we do what we do best - sleep. It stays like this until middle afternoon. In the morning Officer Barton puts in a video he taped about the 9/11 attack on the Twin Towers. I cried of course. It's so heart wrenching to see thousands of people die right before your eyes as the towers collapse. No matter how many times I see it, it always has such an impact on me. I pray for those who died in this attack and for their families. I pray also for the souls of addicts who have died due to this terrible addiction and I thank God for saving my life that I might spend my life being His obedient servant.

I hope my kids are having a good day off school. I'm sure they are going to a cookout somewhere and I hope they're having a blast. They deserve joy. I love them so much.

During the video of the Sept. 11th attack on the World Trade Centers the women voice their opinion that President Bush had knowledge of the attacks and could have prevented it, that the decline of the economy is all Bush's fault, that we should just blow up Afghanistan, and none of this would have happened if Al Gore was president. A true group of Democrats. They ask me what I think. "There is no way I am going to get into a political debate when I am the only Republican in a group of staunch Democrats." Karen says smiling, "Well then we win." "That's the only way you could, " I retort back at her. I'm relieved that she gives up at this point. One thing I have learned in jail is that you can't back down from a verbal war, even if it's not a logical argument.

When Officer Barton brings our lunch I thank him for the video. He tells me he has just reenlisted for the next 13 years. He is in the reserves and is up to getting called for active duty. He is very committed to serving our country and he is anxious as he puts it to get in some "trigger time." Spoken like a true firearm specialist. He says that there is no one here who would care if he left. I believe he's feeling the oblivion I am familiar with and trying to tell me something at the same time, but I don't take the bait. I tell him I'm glad that this country has committed men like him and leave it at that.

Lunch was the best we've ever had-a soybean burger and even with a bun! Also we had macaroni salad, baked potato, (it was rather shriveled up) and a brownie. It was the first time I've eaten my whole meal. I'm sure I've lost weight in here, but I'm not sure how much. That's a good benefit though! I'm so full now I think a nap is in order.

The guard comes with a list of names and tells everyone without a High School diploma to line up, as there is someone from the G.E.D. School here to talk to them. I am the only person out of 22 inmates who does not get up. The guard rudely yells at me, "Blondie, get your ass up and get in this line." Karen jumps in, "Hey, she's smart she don't need no stinkin' G.E.D." The guard gets right in my face, "So how smart are you, do you have your G.E.D. or not Blondie?" Obviously, he was expecting a negative answer. "No," I replied, "I do not have my G.E.D." The guard smiles. "I have my Bachelors degree in International Business from Miami University." The smile disappears from his face as all the girls are laughing hilariously. Nothing pleases them more than when a guard gets put in his place.

So now I know; I am the only blue eyed, blond, suburban housewife, Republican with higher education in this dorm. Does this make me special or different - absolutely not. We are all just women, made by God, locked up in this jail, trying to figure out why we are here.

Tuesday, May 28, Day Fourteen

I have been here two weeks today. As the girls say, "I've got seven days and a wake up left." I am still really dizzy. I'm beginning to think it's the air in here. There's no fresh air and it's very humid from the showers going all the time. The only vent is about 15 feet up on the beige cider walls and it is filled with filth. Everything in this room is painted beige, the bunks, the walls, the ceiling, and the tables. Only the floor, that I call home these days, is not beige, it is just plain old cement. The room is decorated with makeshift clotheslines made of torn sheets and underwear, socks, and bright orange shirts are hanging everywhere.

We received razors today. What a welcome sight. It felt great to shave for the first time in two weeks! For a daily shaver, that's a long time to go. We have to sign the disposable razors in and out and if they don't get them all back we go on lockdown until it's found. Karen thought she had lost hers this morning and almost had a heart attack! Luckily, she found it before anyone knew.

After that, the guard delivered new Bibles from the Chaplain to everyone who went to the service. This was very nice of him. I really wish we could get the AA Big Book but they don't have any at this jail. They don't have a library of any kind here. We don't even have AA meetings here. Well, I've heard that there are meetings but you must have a court order to go to them. That pretty much defeats the purpose of the meeting if you are being forced to go. I really need a meeting. I was doing so good since the accident... I've been having a lot of drinking dreams and cravings though without the meetings. It's really hard to stay focused when you hear talk of drinking and drugging all day long. I've been doing my fourth step while I'm here. When I combine it with what I have done back at the apartment, I should be finished with it. I'm anxious to get back into my program and meetings and start working my fifth step with my sponsor when I get out. I know I'm backsliding in my program while I'm here, but I'm ready to dive right in when I get out.

One suggestion in AA is that you do not get in a relationship for one year. That rule also stands at the "coed" halfway apartment I am in! They don't try and make it easy on you do they? One thing I strongly professed is that my sobriety has to come first but I am not batting a thousand at the relationship thing.

This is totally amazing. I am so excited. I went over to visit on Betty's bed to tell her what I found out from the social worker about her getting into treatment right from here and during our discussion I relate to her my supreme disappointment that we don't have Big Books here or meetings. She smiles at me and produces a brand new Big Book that she got from the Chaplain! It's never been opened and she's letting me borrow it until it's time for me to leave! God is so awesome! Ask and you shall receive. He always takes care of me! I now can redo my fourth step since I have the example. This book will keep me busy until it's my time.

A couple of very nice old ladies from an organization called,

"Companions" came to the dorm and passed out a packet for each person. The packets contained cards, stationary, and five stamped envelopes. How generous. The envelopes I received had no stamps, (only mine were like that) and the commissary has been out of stamps since I got here. You don't have to beat me over the head with a bat. I am not meant to send out letters from here for some reason. I'm just not going to question it. Acceptance is the answer.

We also received new sheets and pants. Ah...the simple pleasures in life I will not take for granted again. This is quite a busy day in the dorm. I received a letter from Collin, and a note from Shar.

Two new girls have arrived at the dorm today. A white girl who looks like Marsha Brady! She has obviously been around the jail circuit a few times, as the women in here know her and are giving her a hard time about being a lesbian. She's tough and handling herself quite well. When she sits down to dinner with Karen and I she starts crying. Even the toughest people in here are hurting. Karen realizes she knows the girl's parents. She won't have to worry about anything. Karen has her back. The other girl is obviously on the revolving door plan. In and out of jail. She is a short, black woman with huge breasts and the wildest hair I've ever seen. When I came to this jail back in February to post my bond she was in the holding cell with me. She kept taking her clothes off and flashing the guard. He finally handcuffed her behind her back to keep her clothes on her. I thought at the time she was just high on cocaine, now I realize she's just a little off mentally. This is not what this dorm needs right now. We are getting way over crowded and I have noticed that racial tensions are rising. You are definitely defined in this jail by the color of your skin, which is one reason why I describe each person that way. I do not consider myself a prejudiced person, and I do get along with everyone fortunately.

Wednesday, May 29, Day Fifteen

Slept all night. Slept all morning. I'm getting so lazy. No one gets up around here until lunchtime because they stay up so late talking. They get up for breakfast and go right back to sleep. I can definitely see why they have developed this pattern. Sleeping helps the day go by faster. I need to start staying awake longer or I am going to be exhausted when I leave here.

Lunch was the exact same thing we had yesterday. Spanish rice and beans, only today, it's more like spicy mush. Rita, a large boned black woman in her late 50's, turns around during lunch and tells me "Blondie, be sure you put this in your journal that they feed dogs better than this crap." Rita is very much the dominant figure in this dorm. She is very aggressive and doesn't take lip from anyone. She has been adamant in vocalizing her view that any show of lesbianism will not be tolerated. She is extremely neat and clean and expects that of everyone else. This is the area of dissention that when the lights go off at night, she wants quiet to sleep. These are the two areas where I see the biggest racial differences and the most tension. The difference being the Black and Mexican side of the room, this is where I sleep, and it is swept and mopped every morning. We also clean the tables and the bathroom every morning. The white half of the dorm refuses to get up and clean, therefore the floor is filled with hair and filth. My side of the dorm wants to go to sleep when the lights go off at 11 or 12 while the white side is just waking up from their after dinner naps and want to laugh and talk and play cards. They actually are quite rude about it too.

Everyone is becoming very interested in what I am writing about because I spend so much time journaling. Many have expressed that they want me to write about them. I tell them to sit down and tell me their story then.

I have become more and more introverted the longer I am here. I'm a very quiet person to begin with and I have never been one for big group girl talks. In fact, I've always gotten along better with men than women. I actually get along best with children though. I don't know what that says about me. I've always had a lot of girlfriends, but I prefer one on one talks. It's pretty obvious that I don't go out of my way to socialize here. Sometimes I feel as though I just want to disappear into the woodwork. I've felt that way my whole life. I've never been one to seek out the spotlight-maybe that's why I always seem to get so much unwarranted attention. I just don't know.

Went to see the doctor today. He is so nice. He checked my foot and my neck and I told him about my dizziness. The nurse took my blood pressure and it was perfect. The doctor said, "either you have an inner ear problem or you're pregnant!" I explained that I did have an inner ear problem after my car accident but it went away in February. As far as being pregnant, every child is a gift from God and I would love to be pregnant someday, but now would be really, really bad timing. Anyway, I think the doctor just really wanted to see how I am doing. He's very caring.

Five new girls have walked in the door tonight. There is no more room in here. I'm beginning to feel very claustrophobic in here. I feel like it is so hot in here and I can't move or breathe well. I feel like everyone on the outside has forgotten about me and I'm all alone. My mind never shuts off and I can never sleep with all this noise. I don't even have any tears left. I feel that everything I've been working so hard for is slipping away; my recovery program, my relationship with my kids, my friends. I must have faith that God will restore these things.

Thursday, May 30, Day Sixteen

While I've been here I've been reading Life Strategies by Dr. Phillip C. McGraw. He has his own show every week. It has been an excellent read especially for where I am at in my life. This is the book Officer Barton gave me my second day here. The book is about taking an honest appraisal of your life; your whole life-every aspect. The process is to be accountable for what you have done, take a critical look at all these dimensions, determining the ideal life you are striving for, setting goals, developing a Life Strategy and finally taking action. I'm at the point now where I am developing my Life Strategy. My major short term goal right now, when I get out, will be to get my recovery program back on track and reconnect with my kids, not to mention finishing my DUI sentence. My long-term goals are keeping my spirituality and sobriety as my first priority because without them I have nothing. Beyond that I want to start building a life for my boys and me. To do this there are so many goals I need to set. I need to get a job, to be able to support us. I need to get moving on this divorce and custody case. I need to find a nice home for us to live in. I need to work on getting my driver's license back. I need to continue working on the 12 steps and keep in constant contact with God. I think this is a great time for some honest self-appraisal.

One of the new girls came over as I was sitting at the table. She said "Everybody keeps telling me to come talk to you because you know all about treatment and stuff." "I've been to treatment and to AA and to a halfway house, so I suppose I know a little about it, but why don't you tell me what got you here first." She's an absolutely beautiful 31-year-old woman with an eleven-year-old daughter and a husband she is divorcing. She's had a life of drinking and drugging and she's tired of it. She, like me, wants a better life for her daughter and herself. She had gotten a DUI a year ago and spent three weeks in this jail and drug court for two years. In drug court you have to drop (do a urine test), three times a week. After seven months of being clean and sober she came up dirty. She tested positive for alcohol and cocaine. She's going to court tomorrow for sentencing and she'll probably have to do 90 days inpatient treatment. She's never been to treatment so I just explained to her what happens and how it has affected my life so positively. I expressed to her the hard decisions I have had to make and the sacrifices I've made to better my life. She's very concerned about leaving her daughter for that long. We had a long talk about how it is the best for her and her daughter if she gets well and what a wonderful future they can have together. This is a chance for a fresh start. After we spoke she said she felt so much better and really could see the positive slant in her situation. Maybe this is why God sent me here.

Friday, May 31 Day Seventeen

Uncle. I've been punished enough. I've learned my lesson. I don't want any more. I will not drink again! O.K. I give. So let me go. Oh, well. It was worth a try.

The whole dorm did not get our commissary this week. They lost our order so we are all really hungry and many women are cranky about it. I've even begun to eat the breakfast. Well, at least the bread and the fruit. I'm hungry all the time now. I have to force myself to eat something at every meal. I'm still exercising two or three times a day. I do about 300 sit-ups and 100 push-ups, plus a variety of other exercises. I have faithfully been exercising my broken ankle. It seems to be less painful now, but I don't see it getting any stronger. I still cannot lift myself up on my right foot, but I'll keep trying. The doctor has prescribed Motrin for me three times a day and that has helped more than anything has. I can actually walk without limping today. That's a great feeling.

Getting all these women off the floor to clean this morning was very difficult, but necessary. This place gets filthy. Everyone was willing to get up but Karen. She just does not get up before lunch. Well, the place got clean despite her.

The shower was absolutely freezing this morning, but refreshing. My hair looks so terrible. My roots are growing out and this rusty water has turned my hair a dirty blonde color. I desperately need a dye job. My face looks really dry and I seem to have more wrinkles around my eyes. I always look older when I get too thin and I really need to drink more fluids. I am getting very dehydrated. I still have my tan though; it has not totally faded. I hear it has been in the 80's and sunny the last few days. I can't wait to feel the sun on my face.

We had the same thing for lunch and for dinner today, chili mac. What is up with that?

I get to see my male friend tomorrow-yeah! I really look forward to that.

I think I have finally realized why I was sent here. I actually knew why I was going here before I came but I thought it was egotistical of me to admit it. I've been sent here to give these women hope and to show them the way to a bright and happy future. Each one of these women has such a great spirit and I see in them such potential; every single one of them. No matter how far down the scale they have gone they deserve a chance at a good life. I spend my day talking to different women, one on one. I don't leave my mat; they just come to me. God is definitely guiding my words because I am no counselor. I encourage them to tell me about themselves by telling them my story honestly. I tell them what I used to be like, what happened, and how happy I am with my newfound life, God and with AA. I accept that I am right now exactly where God wants me to be and where I need to be and I am determined to make the best of it. Then I truly listen to these women and give them the message that they are a good person and God only wants the best for them. They deserve a great life and I encourage them not to settle for less because they deserve the best. A petite, Mexican girl everyone calls Cottontail dissolved into tears when I told her this. She's 27 years old and has been in jail 13 times. She said her dream is to be a professional dancer and rap artist. We discussed some goals she needs to pursue when she gets out of here-staying clean, going to meetings, going to church, living at a shelter instead of on the streets-and I believe anything is possible for her. I tell her what I tell everyone-try this new way of life for six months-if you don't like it, you can go back to drinking and drugging. That life will always be there waiting for you. There is one woman who has been here for four days and has not spoken a word to anyone. She came up next to me in the bathroom while I was combing my oh so gorgeous hair, and just started sobbing. She just couldn't hold it in anymore. I turned around and took her into my arms and just held her. Everyone in the dorm stares at us when these outbursts happen because these are seemingly very tough women breaking down. I have come to accept it as a God thing that they come to me. We stood in the bathroom for quite a while as she told me her story. She's been in drug court for two years and keeps dropping dirty so the judge gave her two weeks in jail. They took her baby while she's here. She has so much to live for. She's been in rehab a couple of times, but as I explained to her, rehab or any kind of treatment is not a cure. If you come out of it and do not change anything then what is the point? If nothing changes, nothing changes. You have to turn your life over to God, you must change your thinking, and behavior and lifestyle and you must get rid of people, places and things associated with your using. These are non-negotiable. They are not my ideas they are fact! The wisdom I pass on to these women I possess because it has been so generously given to me in the rooms of AA. The courage I possess is the direct result of a loving God and the prayers of many friends and prayer groups.

Saturday, June 1 Day Eighteen

The promises written in the Big Book of Alcoholics Anonymous are materializing for me. I always had faith that they would. The promises state:

"If we are painstaking about this phase of our development, we will be amazed before we are half way through. We are going to know a new freedom and a new happiness. We will not regret the past nor wish to shut the door on it. We will comprehend the word serenity and we will know peace. No matter how far down the scale we have gone, we will see how our experience can benefit others. That feeling of uselessness and self-pity will disappear. We will lose interest in selfish things and gain interest in our fellows. Self-seeking will slip away. Our whole attitude and outlook upon life will change. Fear of people and of economic insecurity will leave us. We will intuitively know how to handle situations, which used to baffle us. We will suddenly realize that God is doing for us what we could not do for ourselves."

Right now that happiness is the part that stands out in my mind. I'm actually happy and I'm in jail. How could that be? It is because I've set my mind to making the best out of a bad situation and I am determined to use my experience to help others. I can see now how fortunate I have been and how God is working in my life. It is now time for me to give back some of what has been so freely given to me. Isn't it funny how in helping other women I get such joy? I feel the reason I can be helpful is because I've felt the hopelessness and the despair that they feel. I know what it is like to have no self-esteem and feel worthless and I know what it is like to want help and not know how or where to ask for it or to even feel as though I deserve help. I especially know what it is like to feel so lonely and desperately, with nowhere and no one to turn to. I was so apathetic I did not care if I woke up in the morning and I felt the boys would be better off without me. That's what I mean by the promises are coming true. My whole attitude and outlook upon life has changed. My life is not easy right now by any means, I mean for heaven's sake-I'm in jail, I'm getting a divorce, and I'm not with my children but, that's looking at my life through negative eyes. On a more positive note, I have God as my constant companion. I'm getting a divorce! I have three healthy happy kids that I get to see soon, a loving and supportive family (especially my best friend, Deb), a loving companion, great sober friends, a sponsor, and a killer outlook on life! How could I fail with all that support behind me? I'm destined to succeed at whatever I put my mind to and I won't let anyone or anything stand in my way.

Sunday, June 2 Day Nineteen

Last night was not the best evening I've had. I was looking forward to my evening visit but no one showed. I was pretty disappointed. If the visiting area was full they might not have gotten a time slot, but I have the feeling that they had other plans. There's not much I can do about it. There were a lot of things that I wanted to know about before I left here. The women in here call me Barbie doll. They now want to kick Ken's butt for not showing up! They saw how depressed I was and I think they mean it. I told them I am sure he had a good reason but their attitude is - he's a man, he's probably out there with some other woman, because no man can go three weeks without a woman. That did not make me feel better.

Then the verbal wars began. We got a new woman in here with a loud mouth and a bad attitude. It only takes one person like that in this mix to set things off. There's already tension. I don't believe that women naturally mix as well as men do when just thrown together. The fights are always very long because no one wants to back down and lose face in front of everyone. They're also very vulgar and crude with a lot of profanity and personal attacks. They are always very childish in nature and quickly lose their entertainment value with the crowd. These verbal attacks went on till about 1 a.m. last night and started again this morning at 6 a.m. I couldn't get to sleep after they ended so I probably got about three hours sleep.

I woke up this morning to my daily prayers. I always thank God for waking me up and for my day then I pray for my kids and this morning I prayed for my neighbors. My little boys are at church right now with their dad. I'm so glad he takes them faithfully. I hope we have services tonight. I would really like to go and receive communion but I realize now God is coming to see me in many different forms.

Having not slept well last night I decided to take a nap after lunch. Just as soon as I got into a deep sleep they woke me up saying I have a visit. My roommates Sue and Lisa were here. Lisa looked so pretty in her white summer sweater and black print skirt. Sue looked very fit with her tan and pink sports outfit. We call her sporty spice. Lisa looked quite nervous. She does not adjust well to difficult situations and has been in prison before. I was afraid if she came to visit me that she might have flashbacks as she has Post Traumatic Stress Disorder. But she's a trooper and she came anyway. What a great roommate she has been. She's been taking care of my personal things since I've been gone. I knew I could rely on her. She's very dependable.

Well, they gave me the news about our other roommate, Danielle. Memorial weekend she went back to Lexington with her boyfriend, Jason, to check on her clothing stores. While there, Jason left for two days and relapsed on heroin. He had sold Danielle's car, a brand new Jag, and nearly bankrupted her business. When he came back he brought a bunch of cocaine with him, which Danielle in turn relapsed on. Sue drove to Lexington to pick Danielle up and on the way back Jason kept threatening to kill himself. When they got back to Chicago, Danielle packed her things and flew back to Kentucky.

I just cried and cried when I heard this. I hate this disease and I hate the sick life Danielle and Jason are living and I hate the fact that I'm in here and there is not one thing I can do about it. She was so lively; I'm really going to miss her. I don't want to get close to my roommates any more. It's too hard when they relapse.

I asked them why my male friend didn't come to visit me. They said he worked on Saturday and that he had things to do before I came home on Tuesday. I told them I don't come home till Wednesday, which they knew. They said that they have hardly seen him and that he has just not been himself. I hope everything went okay with his mother's surgery and with him. Maybe he is just depressed.

Lisa sounded like she's doing pretty good and Sue sounded like she is having some financial problems and she's lonely but she's hanging in there. I'm so proud of both of them. Their visit was nice but upsetting to me. I'm so helpless in here.

I've been reading a lot in the Big Book and I've highlighted the most important parts of the book for Betty to read when I'm gone. Whether or not she does is up to her, but she seems to really want it.

I helped Cotton write a letter to the Chaplain explaining to him she would like to get on the waiting list to live in his shelter. I hope this works out for her.

Tonya finally got the home-monitoring device on her ankle and got to leave. She doesn't know if she's being charged with the four felonies for false identification though. She's supposed to call me this weekend and let me know when she's leaving for treatment. She asked me to be her temporary sponsor. I told her I would be glad to help her any way I can until she gets to treatment. I only gave her and Gloria my phone number. Everyone else I just gave the address at the half way office. You never can be too careful.

Thank you God for sending me here and letting me be helpful but I'm ready to go home now!

Monday, June 3 Day Twenty

If I had to do one thing different this year I would have asked my Pastor from my Church to visit me in treatment and here in jail. I could use some good spiritual guidance. I'm not trying to do this by myself anymore. I know I need all the help I can get and I am no longer afraid to ask for it.

I started my period today. We, of course, have no tampax in the dorm. We always run out. So one lady, a very nice, very humorous, woman went around and collected about eight pads for me. This is just another humbling experience - begging the guard to bring us pads every time he opens the door. He just ignores our requests. He has a seriously bad attitude. Everyone seems very cranky today.

I called Mom and Dad. Last time I called Dad was on a fishing trip so I missed talking to him. Luckily they were both home. Unfortunately, while we were on the phone a very loud fight broke out and I couldn't hear them. I told them not to worry, it's like this all the time that I'm used to the noise by now and it's never directed towards me. Mom was worried and told me to stay away from "those women." It's not like they are going to steal my lunch money or something! In fact, everyone here has been quite respectful towards me. They even apologize if they swear when they are talking to me. I can honestly say I have no problems in here, as I explained to my parents. The living conditions are horrible, but tolerable. I've been fine in here as a result of what I've been through this year. I've become accustomed to change, tolerant of all kinds of individuals, flexible with each situation and learned restraint of tongue. I've adopted a kind of go with the flow attitude that is working, so why change it.

I'm craving some kind of security in my life. I want to live in a place I can make my home. A place the boys can call home too! I want to live in one place more than a couple months and I am planning on working hard to achieve this goal when I leave here.

It's going to be weird when I get out of here. I told my roommates Lisa and Sue that I might have to sleep on the floor with a rock for a pillow for a few nights just to feel at home. I won't know what to do when I go out to lunch with Deb and they give me a knife and fork. I'll just have to tell the waiter "Oh, no, thank you, I'll just use this spoon to cut my meat. You can have those weapons back!" Every time I leave my apartment I'll have to assume the position for a pat down.

Tuesday, June 4 Day Twenty One

My last full day here. Let's hope it's uneventful. It's been pouring outside for the last two days. I hope it clears up tomorrow for my little boys softball game.

It's my last evening here. I have no mixed emotions about leaving. I want out. I'm getting very excited. I can't wait to breathe fresh air and just enjoy God's beautiful world. I hope I never take things for granted again.

I wish Gloria were leaving with me. She does not belong here.

I don't think I have written about Gloria yet. I never thought I would come to jail and make a friend, but I'm glad I have. Gloria got arrested early one morning when her car broke down and she was walking down the highway with her two little girls. To make matters worse, she was in her pajamas. She was arrested on a warrant from another state, for failure to appear in court. She had been arrested for giving her employee discount card to a friend to use while working at a department store. She got fired and had a $1,000 fine to pay. She had paid $500 of it but did not have the other $500, so she did not go to court. Hence, the warrant. She has been in this jail for eleven days now-they had told her that Idaho had ten days to come pick her up or she would be released and they have yet to release her. I think it is atrocious that she has spent so much time in such a miserable jail for a misdemeanor. She had just moved to Chicago to her mother's house with her two little girls from Idaho. She had every intention of paying her fines when she got a job. She has two jobs waiting for her if she gets out of here before they fill the positions. She is a spiritual woman of 29 years who knows her Bible well. I can tell she was raised in a very Christian atmosphere. She's very well spoken and has such a cute personality. She sleeps on the floor next to me on the other side of the doorway. I do feel like I'm not going through this alone since she's been here because she is not accustomed to people that talk like this either. She cried for three days straight when she got here but now she has become quite the trooper. I'm really glad I met her and we plan on getting together when we get out. I think she would be a very good influence on me. She's been divorced for five years. She got married when she was 15 years old. She also has a 14-year-old son, who lives with her ex-husband, so she understands what I am going through with my husband, soon to be ex-husband, hopefully.

Wednesday, June 5 Day Twenty Two

Going home today, back to the halfway house. Good-bye to the County Jail, forever.

EPILOGUE

From jail cell to parole! Then life on easy street, right?

One of the hardest, darkest most painful days of my life was the day I drove to Chicago to pick Bridgett up from her 22 DAYS in the County Jail. As I walked down the cement slab leading to the heavy metal door that she was supposed to be exiting from, there was an unbearable stench in the air from the debris littered everywhere. Minutes after I arrived she exited through the door before me. She grabbed me with such force and hugged me till both our bodies fell limp from sobbing uncontrollably. She felt like a bag of bones, and her face was sullen and sunken in. Thankfully, the sun was shining for that brief second in time when she was finally freed from her physical jail cell. I noticed her blonde hair was now orangish, as her eyes tried to adjust to the daylight. The problem was that she had gone into jail strong into her recovery program, (I don't believe she had drank since her car accident,) and she had given out all she had

75

while she was in there. She came out a prisoner to herself once again. I could feel it in her spirit. There are many prisons that tempt us, but let us get one thing straight: God did not put her in that physical jail cell. Although I am sure He used her and the situation to bring joy and hope to those around her. The Good News of the Gospel is that Jesus died to set us free, not put us in prison! Sometimes our prisons are self-inflicted, sometimes they are disciplinary, sometimes they are growth experiences, but regardless, they are used to bring healing passion from our chronic pain and sufferings, comfort to others, or intimacy with God, Himself, and a message from our mess. Somehow I believe God did, is still doing and will continue to do all of these things through Bridgett's journal, 22 DAYS in the County Jail. God loves us unconditionally and uses our experiences to draw us closer to Him.

The Bible says: "He has delivered us from such a deadly peril, and he will deliver us. On him we have set our hope that he will continue to deliver us, as you help us by your prayers." (2 Corinthians 1:10 NIV)

Our prayers had paid off, she came out in one piece without being raped or physically abused. Immediately she wanted to stop at a convenience store to get a Diet Coke and a candy bar, along with some toiletries. Then I took her back to a local motel to shower and rest a bit. You won't believe this, or maybe you will: the next thing she wanted to do was color her hair! Some things just never change! I was glad to see she still cared about something… anything. So I left her to shower, in a private, clean, white bathroom. I think the extreme culture shock hit her at that point in time. When she emerged, looking absolutely beautiful I might add, she wasn't quite sure how to act or react. But then again, I wasn't quite sure what to do or say.

I did what I always do when in uncomfortable circumstances; I pulled out my Bible, and began reading to her. I explained she didn't have to hide anymore and shared the passage that says, "Rather, we have renounced secret and shameful ways; we do not use deception, nor do we distort the word of God." (2 Corinthians 4:2 NIV) Some may think hiding is easier. That is the lie. The truth is that hiding is slow death. Hiding is fear in action, not faith in action. Hiding is the enemy's way of keeping us right where he wants us. I can only imagine the guilt and shame she must have been feeling. But the book of Matthew assures us that "There is nothing concealed that will not be disclosed, or hidden that will not be made known." (Matthew 10:26 NIV) I assured her that God knew everything she was feeling. What would it be like to have your best friend pick you up from jail of all places? To know that your children knew all about why you hadn't made your visitations? To feel like you had let everyone down? Her internal fight was beginning all over again. They don't say the battlefield is in the mind for nothing. I do wish she could have read Joyce Meyer's book, Battlefield of the Mind while she was in prison. It should be mandatory reading for everyone.

Later that afternoon I took her to lunch at a quaint little preppy restaurant in downtown Geneva, outside of Chicago, then we went and got our nails done, ending up at the halfway house that evening.

She was quite a trooper, and handled the day quite well I must admit. What a remarkable woman! I had to laugh when she mentioned how great it was to be given real silverware to eat with at our lunch! "Do you think they'll trust me with a knife?" she kidded.

It was that evening at the halfway house she now called home, that she told me about the journal she kept during her incarceration. She sat on the floor and began reading it to me, slowly and from the beginning. I believe this helped her feel more comfortable, for the jail cell had been her life for what seemed like an eternity. The 360-degree change in one day was a bit much. I am sure the only thing she really wanted was to see her children. However, every time she did try and see them, they were told to stay in their rooms and not to come out or speak to her. They obeyed like good children would, not knowing the full extent of their parents' relationship, but only what was told them by their father. So even if she could have seen them it would only cause her more hurt, more pain, and more discouragement, a bittersweet predicament for sure.

Unfortunately, the next morning I had to head for my home, but I will never forget what she said to me: "Deb, I believe God has put you in my life to help me get my journal published." I smiled and thought to myself, "You have got to be kidding!" Little did I know that it would eventually end up in my hands. God works in mysterious ways.

"Hope deferred makes the heart sick." (Proverbs 13:12 NIV)

Believing that God will do what He has said, is totally different than waiting for Him to do it. That's why people take things into their own hands. People do it every day in one form or another; take things under their own control. Some people give their problems over to God and then take them back.

ONE LAST HEART WRENCHING ENTRY

Before her divorce for some unknown reason, Bridgett pulled out her journal of the 22 days she spent in the County Jail and decided to write one last entry:

April 20th of the following year

It is Easter Sunday and once again I am alone. I was alone last year, am alone this year and the way it looks right now, probably will be next year too. Although with the way God turns my life upside down who knows what the future holds. I wanted to just sleep all day so that it would be over but my back can only take so long in bed. It was aching.

I cleaned my apartment, went on a long bike ride, took a long bath, and made Irish soda bread and cooked a ham. Who knows if I'll actually have a guest for dinner or not, but at least I am prepared if I do. I've called him twice today, but I still don't know if he'll be coming over. He's having a very difficult time dealing with everything

I'm going through. I think worse than I am if that is possible. He has a tendency to run when things get tough. He always comes back though.

I am not going after custody of my boys. I'm so unsure of this decision: I only want to do what is best for them. I know I cannot care for them right now. I am still on probation, I don't drive, and I don't even have an apartment that can hold all of us. I still know they would be better off with me than with a man who would treat his wife of 15 years the way their dad has treated me. To take all the furniture I was to bring back to my apartment and destroy it like he did just shows what a sick, demented mind he has. Not to mention the number of times he has ruined my visitations. How can I leave the boys with someone like that and live with myself.

~~~~~~~~~~~~~~~~~~~~~~~

About a month later, her divorce was finalized. A week later, she received a letter from the court appointed counselor simply stating, "It would be a conflict of interest for me to meet with you and your children." I often wonder if Bridgett read this, and thought to herself, "I cannot go another seven months without seeing or talking to my children, waiting on the courts to appoint a new counselor when I have already given their father custody."

A NIGHTMARE OF AN ENDING

Sometimes days just go from bad to worse; do you know the feeling? The day started out ordinary enough, until the phone rang, then the real nightmare began. It was Memorial Day, May 26, 2003 and this phone call would be the last concerning my best friend. It was from the Chief of Police in her little town in Chicago. "Hello, is this Bridgett's sister?" "Well, we were like sisters," I replied hesitantly. "I am sorry to inform you that your friend took her own life this morning." Your number was on her refrigerator to call in case of an emergency. I dropped to my knees sobbing and praying at the same time.

She left her boys a love letter, and I hope someday they will receive that letter with forgiveness in their hearts for what she has done. The letter was written on the stationery I had given her: "A heart at peace gives life to the body," (Proverbs 14:30 NIV.) Her hope had been deferred so long, that her heart no longer had peace, but was so love sick, that it took her body from life to death. God's

Word is so true when you really look at it. I hope that someday that her boys will come to know their Heavenly Father so that their hearts can be at peace. "God is love." (1 John 4:16 NIV) When we need people to love us, and we come up empty, we can always go God. 1 John goes on to say: "but perfect love drives out fear," (verse 18 NIV.) The same could be said this way: "Fear drives out love." Bridgett's fear, her husband's fear and now possibly their children's fear, will continue to drive out all love until the truth of Who God is really truly sets them free.

The reason I wrote this is as a 'cautionary tale' is so that other women will look at my friend's life, be able to draw strength and courage from her, and remember the wisdom that she forgot so that her life will not be in vain:

"If you come out of it and do not change anything then what is the point? If nothing changes, nothing changes. You have to turn your life over to God, you must change your thinking, and behavior and lifestyle and you must get rid of people, places and things associated with your using. These are non-negotiable." And I would add: remember God's grace is sufficient, that you don't have to do it in your own power. When we quit trusting God, we are walking in our own power, not His and this is when we forget.

So if you read something that was meant to be a caution to you, stop it! Admit it and quit it! If you read something you thought was solid wisdom from above, apply it! But whatever you do never forget that true love is from God above, and He will never fail in the long run, if you only believe!

Her male friend left her, her husband divorced her, and she had lost complete custody of her children. I cannot say that it was easy for her. She definitely carried a cross that I dare not even try to carry myself. But I do know that persistence through faith pays off.

God is in the restoration business, but it takes time. Sometimes lots of time. You cannot be in a hurry, and you cannot set the timeline. You have to believe in the grace of Jesus Christ (that He wants to give you undeserved favors and blessings) and allow Him to be the Savior of your life. He carried the ultimate cross of our sins, so that we could be saved from them and live free of any prison. Follow Him and He will be your husband faithfully. The wages of sin only lead to death, and Christ wants us to live and be His beautiful bride. He will never leave us or forsake us when everyone else does.

I have cried out to God many times throughout this ordeal, "Why?" and He has been gracious enough to answer a few times, but the bottom line always comes down to: So what is love? We have heard it many times in weddings, but listen again with fresh ears and eyes: "Love is patient, love is kind. It does not envy, it does not boast, it is not proud. It is not rude, it is not self-seeking, it is not easily angered, it keeps no record of wrongs. Love does not delight in evil but rejoices with the truth. It always protects, always trusts, always hopes, always perseveres. Love never fails." (I Corinthians 13:4-8) Bridgett and her husband's love failed, but God's love will never fail us. 1 John 4:9 goes on with, "This is how God showed his love among us: He sent his one and only Son into the world that we might live through Him." If you open your heart to His Love today, you will be set free to follow Him. "That if you confess with your mouth, "Jesus is Lord," and believe in your heart that God raised him from the dead, you will be saved. (Romans 10:9 NIV)

God tried to save my friend Bridgett from her depression that miserable day in May. One of the ladies in her apartment complex had invited her to church the day before and actually knocked on the door, but Bridgett chose not to answer, for why, we will never know. God always gives us a choice. I pray that you will make the right choice, for perhaps this is why God sent Bridgett to the County Jail.

The coroner's report said that Bridgett's blood level was absent of any trace of alcohol at her death.

The End.

AUTHOR'S NOTE

*Authors Note: On suicide: taken from Billy Graham's book, Answers to Life's Problems,

To Billy: "A friend told us you said in a column that God would not save a person who committed suicide, no matter what the circumstances were. Our son suffered from a terrible mental problem for years and eventually committed suicide, although I really believe he knew God. What is the basis of your position?" Billy's Answer: "This is not my position. Either your friend misunderstood something in the column or--as sometimes happens because of space limitations-- your newspaper omitted part of the column. I regret very much this misunderstanding. I receive many letters every week from people who are thinking of suicide. I always try to be very careful in answering them, because suicide is a terribly serious matter and I would never want someone to use something I might say as an excuse for committing this terrible act. God gives life to us, and He alone has the right to take it away. Furthermore, even in the midst of very difficult circumstances God is with us when we know Christ, and He can help us gain victory over them. On one hand, therefore, I must stress the fact that suicide is wrong and not part of God's plan. The quote goes on to say: Bible also promises "that neither death nor life...nor anything else in all creation will be able to separate us from the love of God that is in Christ Jesus our Lord" (Romans 8:38) Only one thing will keep us from Heaven, and that is our refusal to turn to Christ in faith and trust. Our good works never save us, because we can never be good enough to earn God's favor. God saves us by His grace alone, as we trust Christ. We must never presume on God's grace or think that it means we can do anything we want without paying consequences. But take comfort in God's grace as you remember your son--and seek to live for Christ each day."

Just because someone takes their own life does not make their life any less important than another. This book is proof positive of that. Remember and don't forget: you are loved.

Suicide is a permanent solution to a temporary problem. Do not give the enemy of your soul the satisfaction. "Faith is being sure of what we hope for and certain of what we do not see." (Hebrews 11:1 NIV) God raised Jesus from the dead after just three days. Give God three sunrises, and see if you don't view your circumstances differently.

If you are being abused please seek help from a local church or organization. If you are contemplating suicide, remember God has a plan for your life and you truly do matter. Have the courage to call the suicide hotline for help:

Suicide prevention lifeline: 1-800-273-8255 or go to your nearest hospital for help. Reach out.

ABOUT THE AUTHOR

Deborah Lovett began as a Women's Ministry Leader in a large church in Ohio. After planning, organizing and teaching for many years, God directed her to begin writing her own studies and her first book, GUSHING SPRINGS. The writing in turn led her to testify to women on God's behalf. She stepped out in faith, churches began calling, and she had found her purpose and hasn't looked back.

Deborah is a God-driven speaker. Her ability to weave humor and real-life experiences into God's Word motivates all who hear to a stronger relationship with Christ. She is a colorful storyteller yet genuine.

The Holy Spirit has taught Deborah how God desires to give us victory in all circumstances. Deborah's passion is to speak to all women about how they can fall in love with Jesus because HE chose them, how to live IN CHRIST, so they can ARISE out of difficult trials through the love, forgiveness and the grace of God. Deborah is best known for her book "ARISE: Out of the Ashes".

She has also written magazine articles for the Alliance Magazine, and has done radio interviews for Sirius XM radio and other blog talk shows as well.

Before ministry Deborah was the Assistant Vice President of Star Bank. She is married and has two adult children and lives in Bellbrook, Ohio.

Deborah's books are available at her website:

www.DeborahLovett.org

You can contact her for speaking events by writing to:

womenofthewell@gmail.com

or by contacting her through her website.

Keep up to date with her on Facebook and Instagram!

Made in the USA
Middletown, DE
11 March 2019